179p

ages 6-10

Harris

Curriculum Laboratory
College of Education
University of Iowa

FLY WITH THE WIND,

FLOW WITH THE WATER

FLY WITH THE WIND,

CHARLES SCRIBNER'S SONS · NEW YORK

FLOW WITH THE WATER

ANN ATWOOD

To Harriet, who moves with grace

Copyright © 1979 Ann Atwood/This book published simultaneously in the United States of America and in Canada
Copyright under the Berne Convention/All rights reserved/No part of this book may be reproduced in any form without the
permission of Charles Scribner's Sons/Printed in the United States of America
1 3 5 7 9 11 13 15 17 19   PD/C   20 18 16 14 12 10 8 6 4 2
Library of Congress Cataloging in Publication Data
Atwood, Ann.
Fly with the wind, flow with the water.
SUMMARY: A collection of haiku, illustrated with color photographs, depicting movement and moving things in nature.
1. Haiku, American. [. Haiku. 2. Nature—Poetry] I. Title.
PZ8.3.A922FI 811'.5'2   79-470   ISBN 0-684-16103-6

This is a book about things
that soar and swing
and leap and run
and tumble and swirl
and flutter and float...

It is a book about things that move:
     clouds and creatures
     trees and grasses
     and of course it is about YOU—
running and jumping and wonderfully belonging
     with everything
     that flies with the wind
     and flows with the water.

One fluttering breeze
and autumn leaves go whirling
in the water-swirl.

Skid boards speeding
    to mix their rings and ripples
        with the flowing foam.

A great wave curling
rolling and hurling
bathers and boats.

Crowds of clouds tumbling

down the smooth sloping slide

of the summer hill.

On a quiet day

a playful breeze keeps trying

to spin a windmill.

The lift of the wind!
Feeling it in the yellow kite
tugging at its string.

High above the hill
a strange giant butterfly
glides among the clouds.

Carnival colors!

The wind keeps changing winners—

a red sail then a blue.

The pelicans
open their
parachute
wings

and
drop
from
the
sky.

For just an instant
leaping off the tree-root—
the feel of flying!

The fishes feeding.
Under their turns and loopings
the water-wiggle.

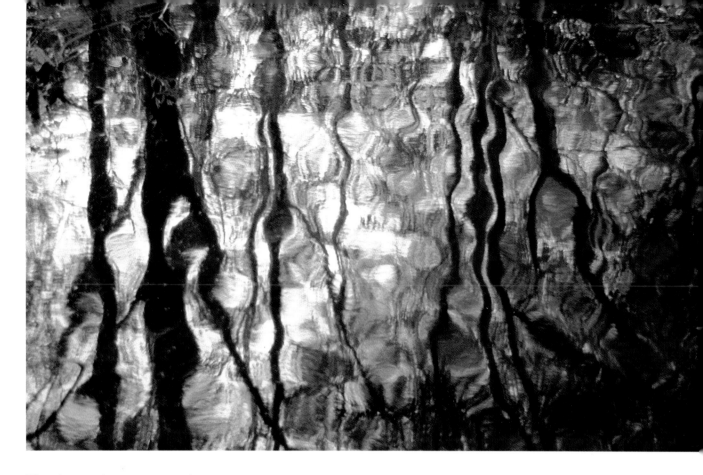

The branches squiggle
in a lake without a wind—
did a duck drift by?

Banners on the bridge...

ducks and

bright reflections

　　　　　swim in the water.

Mischievous piglets
catching the scents of summer
running away again!

The fresh morning air.
In the meadow by the bay
burros are boxing.

Looking straight ahead
going some definite Where—
the geese goose-stepping.

Each time the dog jumps
to catch the flying frisbee
his shadow jumps too.

Excited by the wind
the cat bounds through the grasses
playing jungle games.

Before their final fall
the leaves dizzily waltzing
with the autumn wind.

Small birds swooping down
filling up the branches
of the leafless tree.

One last flash of sun
sending out a signal
and off they streak again...

To fly with the wind
to flow with the water
in a dance of light.